7 days with Dynamic Programming

#7daysOfAlgo

Aditya Chatterjee x Ue Kiao, PhD

Introduction

Dynamic Programming is one of the most important algorithmic domains and is equally challenging. With practice and correct way of thinking, you can master it easily.

We will attempt one problem every day in this week and analyze the problem deeply.

Our schedule:

- **Day 1**: Introduction + Longest Increasing Subsequence
- **Day 2**: 2D version of Day 1 problems
- **Day 3**: Dynamic Programming on Strings
- **Day 4**: Modified version of Day 3 problems
- **Day 5**: Dynamic Programming for String patterns (Longest Palindromic Substring)
- **Day 6**: Modified version of Day 4 problems
- **Day 7**: 2 conditions on 1 data point

On following this routine sincerely, you will get a strong hold on Dynamic Programming and will be able to attempt interview and real-life problems easily.

#7daysOfAlgo: a 7-day investment to Algorithmic mastery.

Introduction is a part of our Day 1 routine where we get the basic idea.

Dynamic Programming is the technique of utilizing the answer of smaller problem set to find the answer of a larger problem set.

$$DP(N_1) = F(DP(M_1), DP(M_2), ..., DP(M_P))$$

where:

- $M_1, M_2, ..., M_P < N_1$
- F is the function of how smaller values $DP(M_i)$ are used

This is the mathematical formulation.

An easily example is the formulation of factorial F(N) where:

F(N) = N! = 1 * 2 * 3 * ... * (N-1) * N

F(N-1) = (N-1)! = 1 * 2 * 3 * ... * (N-2) * (N-1)

F(N) = F(N-1) * N

In this case, calculating F(N) that is N! by the basic formulation requires N-1 multiplication but if we have the answer to F(N-1) that is (N-1)!, then we can find the answer to F(N) that is N! with just 1 multiplication.

This improves the complexity from O(N) to O(1) for this data point.

If you observe carefully, with N-1 multiplications, we can find all values of F(i) for i >= 1 and i <= N. This results in O(N) time complexity.

This is an improvement as with the basic approach finding values of all N values will take $O(N^2)$ time.

The above problem works on one data point. These problems are usually identified as having a formula to directly compute a specific data point.

The use of Dynamic Programming in this case is to generate all such data points sequentially with a better performance. Consider the case of using Dynamic Programming to compute all factorials for 1 to N and you will get the idea.

For the problems which we will explore each day, the advantage of Dynamic Programming lies in finding one specific data point (instead of a range).

Day 1: Longest Increasing Subsequence

We will start with one data point that consists of a set of numerical data and work on a Dynamic Programming solution that will process the 1D data point.

In this problem "**Longest Increasing Subsequence**", we have a set of data and we have to find the longest subsequence which is in increasing order.

Example:

Given set: 1, 9, 19, 17, 32, 15, 99

Longest Increasing Subsequence: 1, 9, 17, 32, 99

Other increasing subsequences are:

- 1, 19, 32, 99
- 1, 19, 15, 99
- 1, 9, 15, 99
- 1, 9, 99

and many more such subsequences.

The brute force approach to solve this is to generate all subsequences, check if the current subsequence is in increasing order and keep track of the longest such subsequence.

The time complexity of this brute force approach is $O(2^N \times N)$ as:

- There are $O(2^N)$ subsequences for N elements

- It takes O(N) time to check if a subsequence is in increasing order

The space complexity is O(1) as we need not store the current subsequence and it can be represented as a bit sequence.

Approach	Time Complexity	Space Complexity
Brute Force	$O(2^N \times N)$	$O(1)$

As this takes exponential time, we must improve it and we can use a Dynamic Programming based approach.

The structure is as follows:

```
dp[i] = Length of Longest Increasing Subsequence
        where the last element is the ith element A[i]
```

The base case is:

```
dp[i] = 1 (by default)
```

This is because a single element satisfies both conditions. Hence, 1 is the minimum answer to our problem.

The recursive relation is:

```
dp[i] = 1 + maximum(dp[j]) where 0 < j < i AND a[j] <= a[i]
```

The answer is the maximum value in the dp array.

We calculate the values in bottom up approach. Following is the pseudocode of our Dynamic Programming approach:

```
dp[0] = 1;

for (int i = 1; i < n; i++)
{
    dp[i] = 1;
    for (int j = 0; j < i; j++ )
        if (a[i] > a[j] AND dp[i] < dp[j] + 1)
            dp[i] = dp[j] + 1;
}
```

The time complexity of this approach is $O(N^2)$ as for the calculation of each value, we go through all previous values.

The space complexity is $O(N)$.

The summary of our time and space complexity is as follows:

Approach	Time Complexity	Space Complexity
Brute Force	$O(2^N \times N)$	$O(1)$

Dynamic Programming	O(N^2)	O(N)

With this, we achieve an exponential improvement.

We will work on a variant of the above problem where we will replace increasing order with decreasing order that is: **Longest Decreasing Subsequence**.

In this problem *"Longest Decreasing Subsequence"*, we have a set of data and we have to find the longest subsequence which is in decreasing order.

The approach is similar to our previous problem "**Longest Increasing Subsequence**".

Example:

Given set: 10, -1, 4, 7, 0, 5, 2, -1

Longest Decreasing Subsequence: 10, 7, 5, 2, -1

Other decreasing subsequences are:

- 10, -1
- 10, 4, 2, -1
- 7, -1
- 10, 7, 2, -1

and many more such subsequences.

The brute force approach to solve this is to generate all subsequences, check if the current subsequence is in decreasing order and keep track of the longest such subsequence.

The time complexity of this brute force approach is $O(2^N xN)$ as:

- There are $O(2^N)$ subsequences for N elements
- It takes $O(N)$ time to check if a subsequence is in decreasing order

The space complexity is $O(1)$ as we need not store the current subsequence and it can be represented as a bit sequence.

As this takes exponential time, we must improve it and we can use a Dynamic Programming based approach.

The structure is as follows:

```
dp[i] = Length of Longest Decreasing Subsequence
        where the last element is the iᵗʰ element A[i]
```

The base case is:

```
dp[i] = 1 (by default)
```

This is because a single element satisfies both conditions.

The recursive relation is:

```
dp[i] = 1 + maximum(dp[j]) where 0 < j < i AND a[j] >= a[i]
```

The answer is the maximum value in the dp array.

Note: the condition a[j] >= a[i] is the difference from the previous problem "Longest Increasing Subsequence".

We calculate the values in bottom up approach. Following is the pseudocode of our Dynamic Programming approach:

```
dp[0] = 1;

for (int i = 1; i < n; i++)
{
    dp[i] = 1;
    for (int j = 0; j < i; j++ )
        if (a[i] < a[j] AND dp[i] < dp[j] + 1)
            dp[i] = dp[j] + 1;
}
```

The time complexity of this approach is $O(N^2)$ as for the calculation of each value, we go through all previous values.

The space complexity is $O(N)$.

The summary of our time and space complexity is as follows:

Approach	Time Complexity	Space Complexity
Brute Force	$O(2^N \times N)$	$O(1)$
Dynamic Programming	$O(N^2)$	$O(N)$

With this, we achieve an exponential improvement.

Day 2: Longest Common Increasing Subsequence

Today, we will work on a modification of our previous problem by extending it to two strings and finding the common maximum answer.

In this problem *"Longest Common Increasing Subsequence"*, we have 2 set of elements and we need to find the longest common subsequence such that the subsequence is in increasing order.

Example:

Given arrays:

a1 = {2,6,4,9}

a2 = {3,4,2,7,9,6}

The answer would be {2, 9} as this is the longest common subsequence which is also increasing.

The brute force approach is to generate all subsequences in the first set S1 of N elements, check if the subsequence in present in the second set S2 of M elements and if the subsequence is in increasing order. We need to keep track of the length of the longest such subsequence.

This brute force approach takes $O(2^N \times (N+M))$ time as:

- There are $O(2^N)$ subsequences in a set of N elements
- It takes $O(M)$ time to check if the subsequence is present in a set of M elements
- It takes $O(N)$ time to check if the subsequence is in increasing order

In terms of space complexity, our brute force approach will take $O(1)$ space as we need not store the subsequence and instead represent it using a bitmap.

We can improve the approach using a Dynamic Programming approach.

Let the two arrays be arr1 and arr2.

The Dynamic Programming structure is as follows:

```
dp[j] = length of Longest common increasing
        subsequence ending with arr2[j]
```

For filling values in this dp array, we traverse all elements of arr1[] and for every element in arr1[i], we traverse all elements of arr2[].

If we find a match, we update dp[j] with length of current LCIS. To maintain current LCIS, we keep checking valid dp[j] values.

The relation is as follows:

```
# if a common element is found in both arrays
if arr1[i] == arr2[j]:
    dp[j] = max(current+1, dp[j])

# if arr1 element is greater, current variable is updated
if arr1[i] > arr2[j]:
    current = max(current, dp[j])
```

Pseudocode

- Creating a dp table of length same as arr2 and elements as 0.
- Start traversing all elements of arr2 for each element of arr1.
- If a common element is found, current variable is incremented and is stored in dp array.
- If element of arr1 is greater than element of arr2, we update our current variable with the maximum of current or the value stored in dp at that index.
- After all elements of arr1 is covered, we return the maximum value from our dp table as result.

The pseudocode is as follows:

```
l1 = length(arr1)
l2 = length(arr2)
```

```python
# creating our dp table that will store the length of LCIS
ending at arr2[j]
dp[l2]

# traversing all elements of arr1
for i from 0 to l1:

    # variable to store length of current LCIS
    current = 0

    # traversing all elements of arr2
    for j in range(l2):

        # if a common element is found in both arrays
        if arr1[i] == arr2[j]:
            dp[j] = max(current+1, dp[j])

        # if arr1 element is greater,
        # current variable is updated
        if arr1[i] > arr2[j]:
            current = max(current, dp[j])

# final result for LCIS
answer = maximum(dp)
```

Example:

Suppose we have arr1 as [2,4,9,1] and arr2 as [2,5,8,4,9,0,1].

Length of both arrays are taken in l1 and l2 variables as l1 = 4 and l2 = 7.

An array with elements as 0 and length same as l2 is declared. Our dp array will look like : [0,0,0,0,0,0,0]

We start traversing all elements of arr2 for each element of arr1.

When we find a common element, we update our dp table at that index and if we find arr1 element greater than arr2 element, we update out current variable accordingly.

After traversing first element of arr1, and all elements of arr2, our dp table will look like : [1,0,0,0,0,0,0] as first element of both arrays were common and current variable at that time was 0.

Similarly, for all elements of arr1, exact process is repeated, our dp table at end would like : [1,0,0,2,3,0,1].

At end, maximum value from this dp table is our answer which is LCIS=3.

The time complexity of our Dynamic Programming approach will be **O(NxM)** with space complexity of O(M).

The summary of the approach is as follows:

Approach	Time Complexity	Space Complexity
Brute Force	$O(2^N \times (N+M))$	$O(1)$
Dynamic Programming	$O(NxM)$	$O(M)$

We will work on a variant of the previous problem by replacing increasing order by decreasing order that is: **Longest Common Decreasing Subsequence**.

In this problem, we have 2 set of elements and we need to find the longest common subsequence such that the subsequence is in decreasing order.

This is similar to our previous problem "Longest Common Increasing Subsequence".

Example:

Given arrays:

a1 = {9, 4, 6, 2}

a2 = {6, 9, 7, 2, 4, 3}

The answer would be {9, 2} as this is the longest common subsequence which is also decreasing. There are other subsequences of length 2 that satisfies the conditions.

The brute force approach is to generate all subsequences in the first set S1 of N elements, check if the subsequence in present in the second set S2 of M elements and if the subsequence is in decreasing order. We need to keep track of the length of the longest such subsequence.

This brute force approach takes $O(2^N \times (N+M))$ time as:

- There are $O(2^N)$ subsequences in a set of N elements
- It takes $O(M)$ time to check if the subsequence is present in a set of M elements

- It takes O(N) time to check if the subsequence is in decreasing order

In terms of space complexity, our brute force approach will take O(1) space as we need not store the subsequence and instead represent it using a bitmap.

We can improve the approach using a Dynamic Programming approach.

Let the two arrays be arr1 and arr2.

The Dynamic Programming structure is as follows:

```
dp[j] = length of Longest common decreasing
        subsequence ending with arr2[j]
```

For filling values in this dp array, we traverse all elements of arr1[] and for every element in arr1[i], we traverse all elements of arr2[].

If we find a match, we update dp[j] with length of current LCDS. To maintain current LCDS, we keep checking valid dp[j] values.

The relation is as follows:

```python
# if a common element is found in both arrays
if arr1[i] == arr2[j]:
    dp[j] = max(current+1, dp[j])

# if arr1 element is greater, current variable is updated
if arr1[i] < arr2[j]:
    current = max(current, dp[j])
```

Pseudocode

- Creating a dp table of length same as arr2 and elements as 0.
- Start traversing all elements of arr2 for each element of arr1.
- If a common element is found, current variable is incremented and is stored in dp array.
- If element of arr1 is smaller than element of arr2, we update our current variable with the maximum of current or the value stored in dp at that index.
- After all elements of arr1 is covered, we return the maximum value from our dp table as result.

The pseudocode is as follows:

```
l1 = length(arr1)
l2 = length(arr2)

# creating our dp table that will store the length of LCDS
ending at arr2[j]
```

```python
dp[l2]

# traversing all elements of arr1
for i from 0 to l1:

    # variable to store length of current LCDS
    current = 0

    # traversing all elements of arr2
    for j in range(l2):

        # if a common element is found in both arrays
        if arr1[i] == arr2[j]:
            dp[j] = max(current+1, dp[j])

        # if arr1 element is greater,
        # current variable is updated
        if arr1[i] < arr2[j]:
            current = max(current, dp[j])

# final result for LCDS
answer = maximum(dp)
```

Example:

Suppose we have arr1 as [1, 9, 4, 2] and arr2 as [1, 0, 9, 4, 8 , 5, 2].

Length of both arrays are taken in l1 and l2 variables as l1 = 4 and l2 = 7.

An array with elements as 0 and length same as l2 is declared. Our dp array will look like : [0,0,0,0,0,0,0]

We start traversing all elements of arr2 for each element of arr1.

When we find a common element, we update our dp table at that index and if we find arr1 element greater than arr2 element, we update out current variable accordingly.

After traversing first element of arr1, and all elements of arr2, our dp table will look like : [1,0,0,0,0,0,0] as first element of both arrays were common and current variable at that time was 1.

Similarly, for all elements of arr1, exact process is repeated, our dp table at end would like : [1,2,2,2,2,2,2].

At end, maximum value from this dp table is our answer which is LCDS=2.

The time complexity of our Dynamic Programming approach will be **O(NxM)** with space complexity of O(M).

The summary of the approach is as follows:

Approach	Time Complexity	Space Complexity
Brute Force	$O(2^N x(N+M))$	$O(1)$
Dynamic Programming	$O(NxM)$	$O(M)$

Note: The approach is same as the previous approach. This is because increasing and decreasing are same class of relative operation. If we consider another class of operation like addition, the approach will change. Think about this.

Day **3**: Longest Common Substring

We will start by analyzing a problem involving 2 strings and how Dynamic Programming can be applied over two data points.

In this problem *"Longest Common Substring"*, we will have two input strings (say str1 and str2) and we need to find the length of the longest substring in the first string (str1) that is present in the second string (str2) as well.

Substring is a contiguous part of the original string. For example, a string S of length L can have a substring of length K where the characters will be S[i], S[i+1], ..., S[i+K-1] where 0 <= i < L and i+K-1 <= L-1.

str1 = opengenus

str2 = genius

Output = gen

The longest common substring of str1 (opengenus) and str2 (genius) is "gen" of length 3.

Let us assume that the length of the input string S1 is N and S2 is M.

The brute force approach will be to check for every possible substring. As there will be $O(N^2)$ substrings in a string of length N and the time complexity of comparing two strings with the smaller length M is $O(N)$, the time complexity of brute force approach will be **$O(N^2xM)$**.

The space complexity of our brute force approach will be $O(1)$ as we need not store the current substring.

We can solve this problem efficiently using Dynamic Programming.

The basic structure is:

```
dp[i][j] = length of the longest substring in
           first i characters of S1 and first
           j characters of S2
```

The basic case is dp[i][j] = 0 if i = 0 or j = 0 or both.

Now if s1[i-1] == s2[j-1], then dp[i][j] = 1 + dp[i-1][j-1], that is result of current row in matrix dp[][] depends on values from previous row. Hence the required length of longest common substring can be obtained by maintaining values of two consecutive rows only, thereby reducing space requirements to 2 * N.

```
dp[i][j] = 1 + dp[i-1][j-1]    if s1[i-1] == s2[j-1]
```

If the length of S1 is N and S2 is M, then our answer is dp[N][M].

The time complexity of the Dynamic Programming approach is **O(NxM)**. This is an improvement by a factor of N which is significant.

The space complexity of our Dynamic Programming approach is O(N).

Approach	Time Complexity	Space Complexity
Brute Force	$O(N^2\text{x}M)$	O(1)
Dynamic Programming	O(NxM)	O(N)

Question: How could you recreate the longest common substring from this data?

Hint: Analyze how the DP values are calculated.

Approach:

Keep track of the first value of i and j where the largest value is stored. We need to backtrack from this point (i=i-1 and j=j-1). This is done in linear time O(N).

Day 4: Longest Common Subsequence

In this problem *"Longest Common Subsequence"*, we have two input strings S1 and S2 and we need to find the length of the longest subsequence that is common to both strings.

Subsequence of a string S is a string P where the order of characters in P is same as the order of characters in S (may not be sequential).

Example:

str1 = opengenus

str2 = engineers

The largest common subsequence can either be "engns" or "enges" as the length of both the subsequences are equal i.e. 5.

This is a variant of our previous problem and will give us deep insights into solving problems using Dynamic Programming as problem statement incrementally changes.

The brute force approach is to generate all subsequences in string S1, check if it is present in substring S2 and keep track of the longest length.

As there are $O(2^N)$ subsequences of a string of length N and comparing two strings with smaller length M takes $O(M)$, the time complexity of brute force approach is $O(2^N \text{ x } M)$.

The space complexity of the brute force approach is **O(N)** as we need to store the current subsequence.

We can solve this problem efficiently using **Dynamic Programming**.

The basic structure of Dynamic Programming approach is:

```
dp[i][j] = Length of Longest Common Subsequence
           with the first ith characters in S1
           and the first jth characters in S2
```

You will notice that this is same as the previous problem. This brings in a deep insight. Observe the difference in calculation.

The basic case is dp[i][j] = 0 if i = 0 or j = 0 or both.

If S1[i-1] = S2[j-1] (when the characters at i^{th} and j^{th} index matches), then set dp[i][j] to 1 + dp[i-1][j-1].

```
dp[i][j] = 1 + dp[i-1][j-1]    if s1[i-1] == s2[j-1]
```

Otherwise, store the maximum value among the following:

- the character S1[i] and S2[j-1]
- the character S1[i-1] and S2[j]

This equates to dp[i][j] = maximum(dp[i][j-1], dp[i-1][j]).

```
dp[i][j] = maximum( dp[i][j-1], dp[i-1][j] )
                if s1[i-1] != s2[j-1]
```

This is because if the current characters do not match, then the maximum length is either the maximum length on moving one character back.

Note: We need not go further back (like moving both character back dp[i-1][j-1]) as this case is covered in the sub-cases.

The time complexity of this approach is O(NxM) while the space complexity is O(NxM).

This is the comparison table:

Approach	Time Complexity	Space Complexity
Brute Force	$O(2^N \times M)$	O(N)
Dynamic Programming	O(NxM)	O(NxM)

The improvement with Dynamic Programming is much clearer with this problem. Analyze this problem along with the previous problem carefully as these are the fundamental pillars of Dynamic Programming.

Day 5: Longest Palindromic Substring

In this problem "Longest Palindromic Substring", we have a string S and we have to find the longest substring in S that is a palindrome.

A substring is a contiguous sequence of characters within a string. For example, in the string "minor"; "in", "ino" and "min" are substrings, but not "mr". Palindrome is a word that reads the same backwards as forwards. Examples include abba, aaaa, hannah.

Consider a string "babad", the longest palindromic substring is "bab". However, "aba" is also a valid answer.

Similarly

aabac --> aba

gogogh--> gogog

Note in the above example ogo is also a palindrome but gogog is the longest one.

The brute force approach to solve this problem is to generate all substrings, check if the current substring is a palindrome and keep a track of the length of the longest palindromic substring.

This approach will take **O(N³)** time complexity as:

- There are $O(N^2)$ substrings in a string of length N

- It takes O(N) time to check if a string of length N is a palindrome
  (Hint: compare first and last characters and so on)

We can improve this with a Dynamic Programming approach.

The structure of our Dynamic Programming approach is:

```
dp[i][j] = whether the substring from index
           i to j is a palindrome or not
```

We shall consider three cases:

- Case 1: 1 character
- Case 2: 2 characters
- Case 3: More than 2 characters

Case 1: i == j (single character)

Every single character of a string is a palindrome. Therefore dp[i][j] is true.

```
dp[i][j] = true
```

Case 2: j-i=1 (2 characters)

We are checking two characters at a time, if s[i]==s[j], then dp[i][j] is
true.

```
dp[i][j] = true if S[i] == S[j]
```

Case 3: j-i>=2 (string with more than 2 characters)

Consider "aba", s[0]=s[2], therefore dp[i][j] will be true. If s[i]==s[j] and
j-i>=2, dp[i][j] = dp[i+1][j-1].

 Now the i+1,j-1 coordinates are literally eliminating the first and last
character, since they are already the same, we want to know if the
string without them is still a palindrome or no? This result will in turn
be any of the above cases or this case, nevertheless, the result has
already been calculated.

```
dp[i][j] = dp[i+1][j-1] if S[i] == S[j]
```

With this, our answer is to maximize the value j-i+1 such that dp[i][j] is
true.

If you analyze closely, you will notice we are only reducing the time
taken to compare strings but utilizing the property of palindromic
strings.

Our complete pseudocode is as follows:

```
for(int i=n-1; i>=0; i--)
{
    for(int j=i; j<=n-1; j++)
    {
        if(i==j)
            dp[i][j] = TRUE;
        else if(s[i] == s[j])
        {
            if(j-i == 1)
                dp[i][j]=TRUE;
            else
                dp[i][j] = dp[i+1][j-1];
        }
        if(dp[i][j] AND j-i >= maximum)
        {
            maximum = j-i;
            X = i;
            Y = j;
        }
    }
}
```

With this, the time complexity becomes $O(N^2)$ and a space complexity of $O(N^2)$.

In practice, our Dynamic Programming approach works well as we need to work on a 2D array of Booleans.

Approach	Time Complexity	Space Complexity

| Brute Force | $O(N^3)$ | $O(1)$ |
| Dynamic Programming | $O(N^2)$ | $O(N^2)$ |

We saw an improvement by a factor of N and a key idea:

When it comes to special strings like palindrome, we can avoid the cost of comparison. Ideally, comparing strings take O(N) time and the usual approach is to convert it to integers and compare it in constant time.

Day 6: Longest Palindromic Subsequence

In this problem, we have a string S and we need to find the longest subsequence in S which is a palindrome.

We have explored the ideas of subsequence and palindrome in previous problems.

For example:

Input string: ABBDCACB

The length of longest palindromic subsequence is 5.

The longest palindromic subsequence is BCACB.

Input string: BBABCBCAB

The length of longest palindromic subsequence is 7.

The longest palindromic subsequence is BABCBAB.

The brute force approach is to generate all subsequences, check if a subsequence is a palindrome and keep track of length of the longest subsequence which is a palindrome.

This brute force approach takes $O(2^N \text{x} N)$ time complexity as:

- There are $O(2^N)$ subsequences in a string of length N
- It takes $O(N)$ time to check if a given string of length N is a palindrome

We can improve this using a Dynamic Programming approach.

The structure is as follows:

```
dp[i][j] = length of the longest palindromic  subsequence
           in substring from index i to j
```

If the ith and j^{th} characters are same, then the longest palindromic subsequence in L[i][j] is same as L[i+1][j-1] + 2. This is because L[i+1][j-1] is for the substring where the ith and j^{th} characters are removed from L[i][j].

```
L[i][j] = L[i+1][j-1] + 2;
```

The other case is that L[i][j] will be the maximum of either of the substring where i^{th} character or j^{th} character is removed.

```
L[i][j] = max(L[i][j-1], L[i+1][j]);
```

With this, our answer will be contained in:

```
L[0][N-1] where N is the length of the original string
```

The pseudocode is as follows:

```
for (i = 0; i < n; i++)
    L[i][i] = 1;

// TOP to BOTTOM
for (i=n-2; i>=0; i--)
{
    for(j=i+1; j<n; j++)
    {
        if (str[i] == str[j] AND j-i+1 == 2)
            L[i][j] = 2;
        else if (str[i] == str[j])
            L[i][j] = L[i+1][j-1] + 2;
        else
            L[i][j] = max(L[i][j-1], L[i+1][j]);
    }
}

answer = L[0][n-1];
```

The time complexity of this approach is $O(N^2)$ with space complexity as $O(N^2)$.

Following is the summary of the time and space complexity of the approaches:

Approach	Time Complexity	Space Complexity
Brute Force	$O(2^N \times N)$	$O(1)$
Dynamic Programming	$O(N^2)$	$O(N^2)$

We achieved an improvement by an exponential factor $O(2^N)$.

Day 7: Longest Increasing Odd Even Subsequence

In this problem, we are an array of N elements and we need to find the longest subsequence such that every alternative element is odd and even starting with odd number and all elements in the subsequence is in increasing order.

Example:

Given array :

arr = {5,6,2,1,7,4,8,3}

Our output will be 4, as {5,6,7,8} is the longest subsequence having alternate odd and even elements.

The brute force approach will be to generate all subsequences, check if the subsequence has odd and even elements consecutively and is in increasing order and keep a track of the length of the longest subsequence that satisfies the condition.

This brute force approach takes $O(2^N \times N)$ time as:

- There are $O(2^N)$ subsequences
- It takes $O(N)$ time to verify if a subsequence is satisfying the condition

So, our Efficient approach would be to use Dynamic programming to solve this problem.

We store the longest increasing odd-even sub-sequence ending at each index of given arr[]. We create an auxiliary array dp[] such that dp[j] stores length of Longest increasing odd even subsequence or LIOES ending with arr[j]. At the end, we return maximum value from this array.

```
dp[j] = length of Longest increasing odd
        even subsequence ending with arr[j]
```

For filling values in this dp array, we traverse all elements of arr[] and for each element, we traverse all elements of same array till that position and check for our conditions.

If it satisfies all the conditions, we update dp[j] with length of current LIOES.

```
if (arr[i] > arr[j] and
      (arr[i]+arr[j]) % 2 != 0 and
      dp[i] < dp[j] + 1)
```

```
dp[i] = dp[j] + 1
```

Pseudocode

- Create a dp table of length same as given array and elements as 1, because each element of given array is a subsequence itself.
- Start traversing all elements of arr and for each element, traverse all the elements till that position again checking for conditions.
- If all the conditions are satisfied, that position in dp[] array is incremented.
- Conditions we check for are : arr[i]>arr[j] and (arr[i] + arr[j]) % 2 != 0 and dp[i] < dp[j] + 1 where, i is iterator of primary loop and j is iterator of secondary loop.
- After our primary loop is completed, we return the maximum value of our dp array.

```python
# Taking length of given array
l = len(arr)

# Creating the DP table of length l and elements as 1
dp[] = [1]*l

# Primary loop
for i in range(1,n):

    # Secondary loop
    for j in range(i):

        # Checking for conditions
        if (arr[i] > arr[j] and (arr[i]+arr[j]) % 2 != 0 and
dp[i] < dp[j] + 1):
```

```
                # Incrementing value in dp table
                dp[i] = dp[j] + 1

# maximum value from DP array
ANSWER = maximum(dp)
```

Workflow of solution

Suppose we have our input array arr1 as [2,7,3,4,9,1].

Length of array is taken in l variable as l = 6.

An array with elements as 1 and length same as l is declared. Our dp array will look like: [1,1,1,1,1,1]

We start traversing all elements of arr and for each element, we traverse same array again till that position.

When we find an element in secondary loop, that is smaller than our current element of primary loop and satisfies the odd-even condition and length of LIOES at that position + 1 is greater that LIOES of current primary loop position than we increment our dp table at that index.

After traversing on second element of arr, and all elements of same arr till second element, our dp table will look like : [1,2,1,1,1,1] as first element of arr satisfies all the conditions mentioned above, we incremented the our dp table at second position.

Similarly, for third elements of arr, exact process is repeated, and as first element again satisfies all conditions our dp table would look like: [1,2,2,1,1,1]. Here we incremented our third element of dp array.

After our primary loop is completed, our dp table would look like: [1,2,2,3,4,1]

At end, maximum value from this dp table is returned by function as our LIOES=4.

Complexity of our Dynamic Programming approach

As we traverse all elements of arr twice in a nested loop, our time complexity would be $O(N^2)$, where n is length of array.

For storing all LIOES for each element of arr, we created an array of size N, so our space complexity would be $O(N)$.

The summary of time and space complexity is as follows:

Approach	Time Complexity	Space Complexity
Brute Force	$O(2^N x(N))$	$O(1)$
Dynamic Programming	$O(N^2)$	$O(N)$

This is an important problem as we have considered multiple conditions for our subsequences. Notice how it changed the solution structure and recursive relations. Think over it.

Conclusion

With the last 7 Dynamic Programming problems in the last 7 days, you must have a good hold on Dynamic Programming by now.

Before an Interview, revise these 7 core problems quickly so that you get into the problem-solving mindset and you can solve challenging algorithmic problems easily.

Follow the following steps:

- Define a problem statement and come up with a Dynamic Programming solution.
- Analyze the performance with other approaches.
- Modify the problem statement slightly and see how the Dynamic Programming approach is modified.

These bring out the true insights of an algorithmic problem.

Remember:

Dynamic Programming is an approach to find answer to larger problems by using answers to smaller problems.

It **reduces the search space** significantly.

 iq.opengenus.org

 discuss.opengenus.org

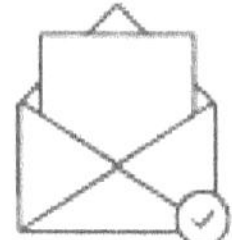 team@opengenus.org

 amazon.opengenus.org

 linkedIn.opengenus.org

 github.opengenus.org

 twitter.opengenus.org

 facebook.opengenus.org

 instagram.opengenus.org

---

Feel free to get in touch with us and enjoy learning and solving computational problems.